Little Lady's
Adventure
in Alphabet Town

by Janet Riehecky
illustrated by Jodie McCallum

created by Wing Park Publishers

CHILDRENS PRESS ®
CHICAGO

Library of Congress Cataloging-in-Publication Data

Riehecky, Janet, 1953-
    Little Lady's adventure in Alphabet Town / by Janet
Riehecky ; illustrated by Jodie McCallum.
        p.   cm. — (Read around Alphabet Town)
    Summary: Before going out to lunch, the little lady searches
for objects that start with the letter "L." Includes activities.
    ISBN 0-516-05412-0
    [1. Alphabet—Fiction.   2. Lost and found possessions—
Fiction.] I. McCallum, Jodie, ill. II. Title. III. Series.
PZ7.R4277Ld   1992
[E]—dc 20   91-20542
                                                              CIP
                                                              AC
                                                              Rev.

Little Lady's
Adventure
in Alphabet Town

You are now entering Alphabet Town,
With houses from "A" to "Z."
I'm going on an "L" adventure today,
So come along with me.

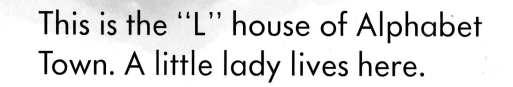

This is the "L" house of Alphabet
Town. A little lady lives here.

The little lady likes "l" things.
She has lots of them.

The little lady has

lovebirds,

lambs,

lilies and lilacs.

She also has

lollipops, lots and lots of lollipops.

Because the little lady has so many
"l" things, sometimes some of them
get lost.

One day, the little lady was invited out for lunch. She put on a lacy dress, but she could not find her lipstick.

"Lemonade and lollipops," she said. "Where can it be?" She looked and looked. Guess where she found it?

She found the lipstick in her jar of

licorice.

12

Then the little lady put on her shoes, but her shoe laces were missing.

"Lemonade and lollipops," she said "Now where can they be?" She looked and looked. Guess where they were?

They were in her jar of

lemon sticks!

Then the little lady looked for her locket. But it was lost too.

The lady looked and looked. At last she saw it—high up where she kept her lemonade jug.

"I'm too little to reach it,"
she said. "But I know. I will

lasso   it."

The little lady swung the rope.
But did she lasso the locket? No,
she lassoed the lemonade jug.

"Lemonade and lollipops," she said.
"What can I do now? I know," she said.
"I will get something to climb on."

She made a tower with a

lunchbox,

a   lamp

and a log.

But when she climbed on top, she was still too little to reach the locket.

"I need something larger," she said.
She looked outside and saw a

lawn
chair.

"That will do," she said.

So she put the lawn chair on top of
the lunchbox, the lamp and the log.

But she was still too little—and
the tower started to lean.

"What will I do?" said the little lady. "I know, I will get my little

lifeboat."

She put it on top of the tower. Then she climbed on top.

She could almost touch the locket. But just then the tower leaned. It started to fall.

The little lady leaped for the locket and LANDSLIDE.

The little lady got her locket,
but she also got a lump on her leg.

"Well," she said. "At least I will
not be late for lunch." She put on
her locket and started to leave.

But at the door, she looked back
at the mess. "Next time," she said,
"I think I will use a ladder."

MORE FUN WITH LITTLE LADY

What's in a Name?

In my "L" adventure, you read many "L" words. My name begins with an "L." Many of my friends' names begin with "L" too. Here are a few.

Louis

Lauren

Larry

Lynn

Lyndon

Linda

Do you know other names that start with "L"?
Does your name start with "L"?

Little Lady's Word Hunt

I like to hunt for "l" words. Can you help me find the words on this page that begin with "l"? How many are there? Can you read the words?

pillow

lion

doll

ball

juice

lemon

dollar

lightbulb

Can you find any words with "l" in the middle?
Can you find any with "l" at the end?
Can you find a word with no "l"?

Little Lady's Favorite Things

"L" is my favorite letter. I love "l" things. Can you guess why? You can find some of my favorite "l" things in my house on page 7. How many "l" things can you find there? Can you think of more "l" things?

Now you make up an "l" adventure.